WORLD AND REGIONAL OUTLINE MAPS

HOLT, RINEHART AND **WINSTON**
Harcourt Brace & Company
Austin • New York • Orlando • Atlanta • San Francisco • Boston • Dallas • Toronto • London

CONTENTS

*T*he *World and Regional Outline Maps* workbook is a valuable resource that enhances teaching flexibility in the classroom. In this workbook, you will find 25 outline maps. Most are map outlines of various regions of the world, and two world map projections are included. You also will find a variety of special maps in this workbook, including world climate regions, world time zones, and plate tectonics.

These outline maps are designed to allow flexibility in the classroom. The pages are perforated, so the outline maps can be removed from the workbook and photo-copied for use in the classroom. Most labels have been deleted from these outline maps, allowing you to use the maps in many ways. For example, students might use them to label countries or regions, to highlight special features, or to identify important concepts and characteristics.

This workbook, with its variety of uses, is an excellent complement to the rest of your program.

Name _____   Class _____   Date _____

OUTLINE MAP 1

The World: A Robinson Projection

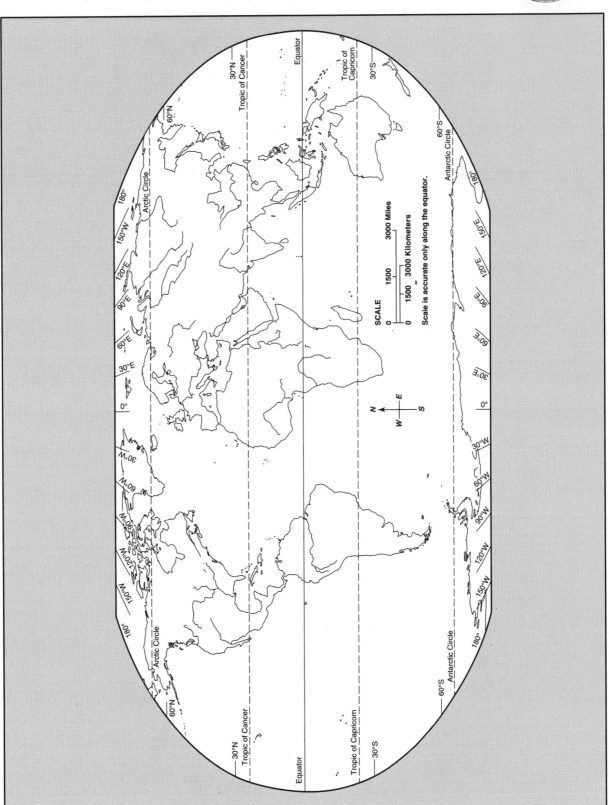

Name _____ Class _____ Date _____

The World: A Mercator Projection

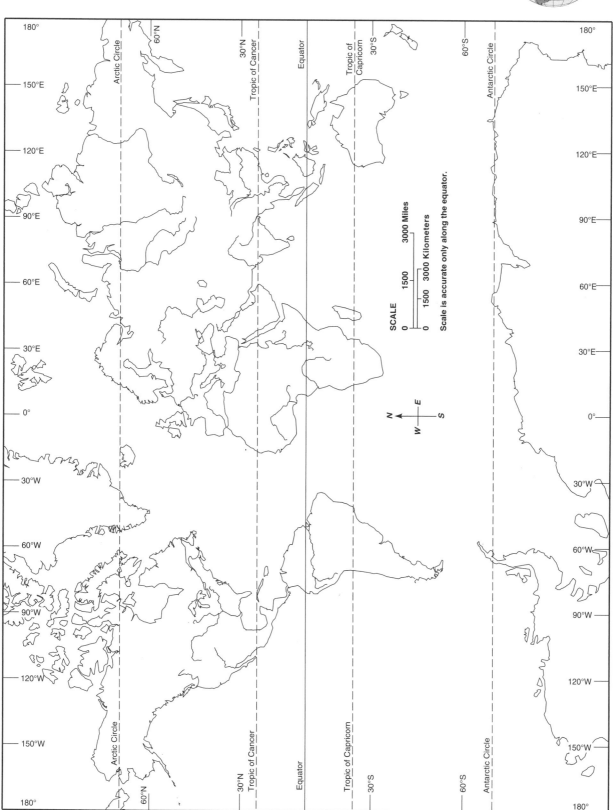

SCALE

0   1500   3000 Miles

0   1500   3000 Kilometers

Scale is accurate only along the equator.

N
W — E
S

OUTLINE MAP 3
The Drifting Continents

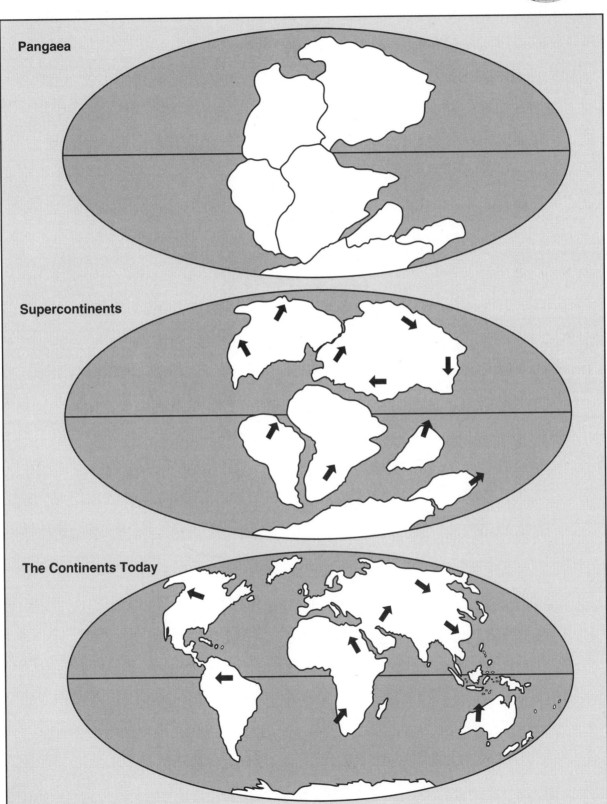

Pangaea

Supercontinents

The Continents Today

OUTLINE MAP 4

Plate Tectonics

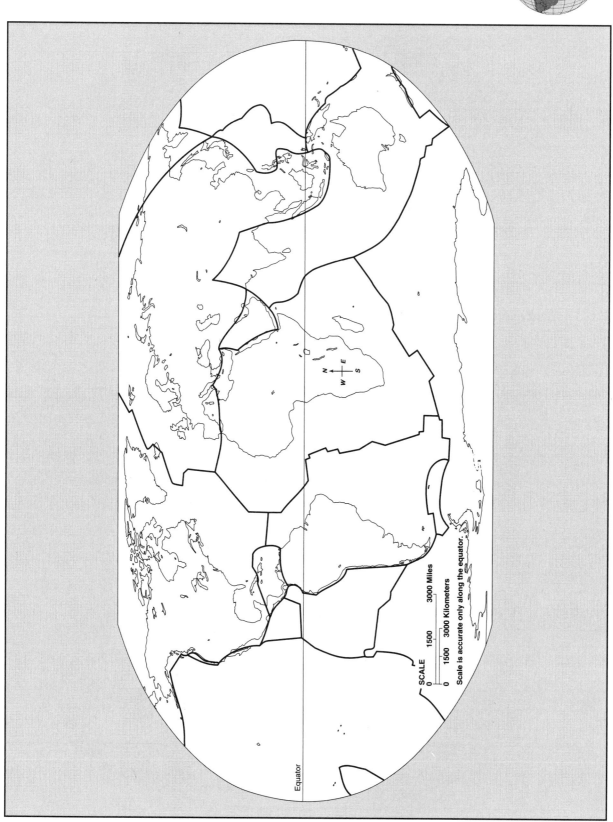

SCALE

0   1500   3000 Miles

0   1500   3000 Kilometers

Scale is accurate only along the equator.

Equator

Name _____ Class _____ Date _____

OUTLINE MAP 5

World Time Zones

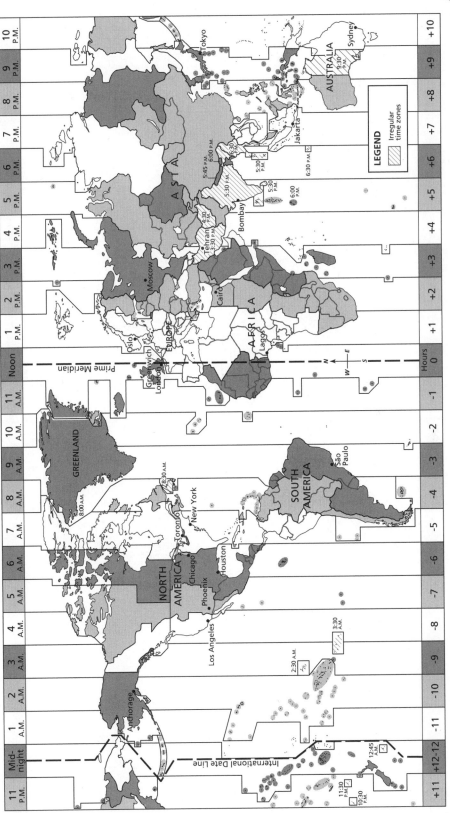

OUTLINE MAP 6

World Climate Regions

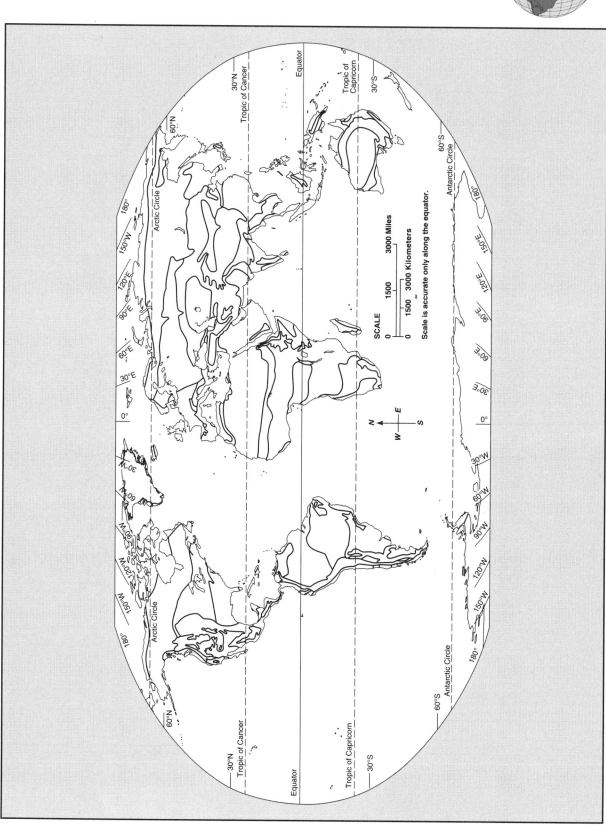

SCALE

0   1500   3000 Miles

0   1500   3000 Kilometers

Scale is accurate only along the equator.

OUTLINE MAP 7

Physiographic Regions of the United States and Canada

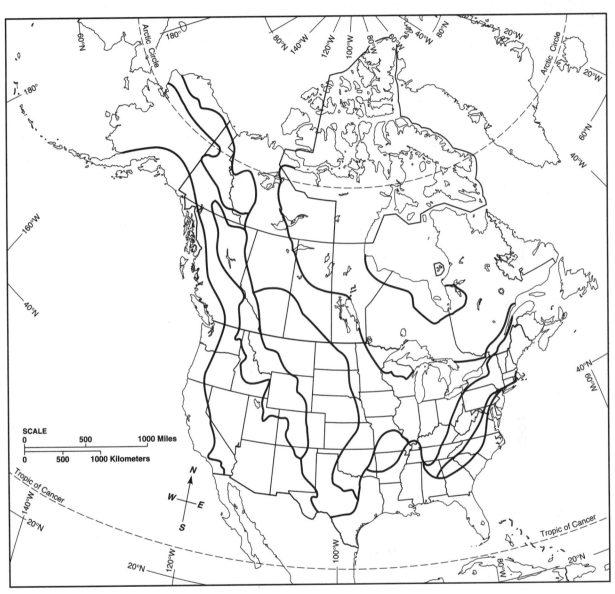

OUTLINE MAP 8

North America

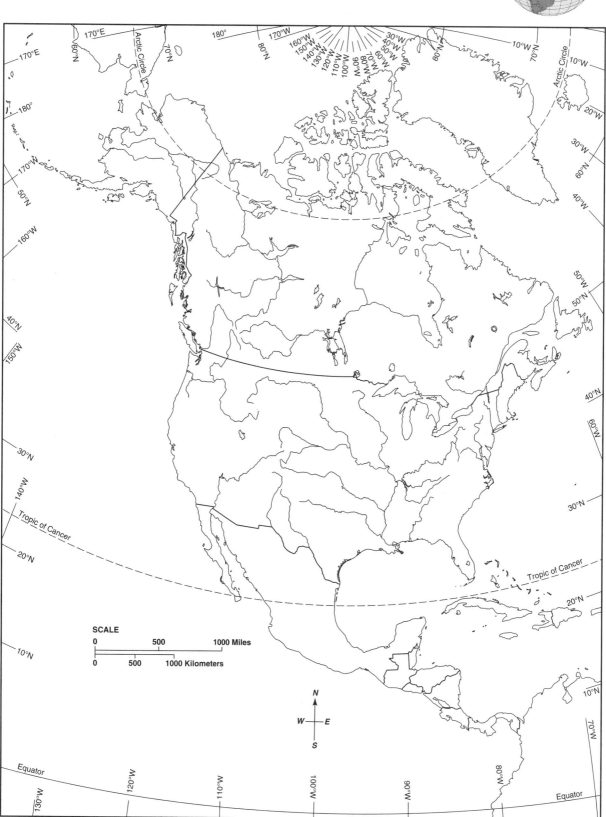

SCALE

0 — 500 — 1000 Miles

0 — 500 — 1000 Kilometers

OUTLINE MAP 9

The Contiguous United States

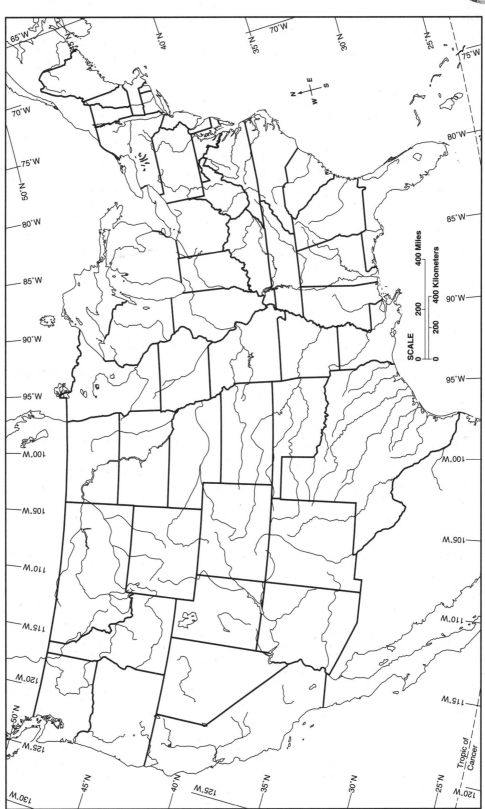

Name _____ Class _____ Date _____

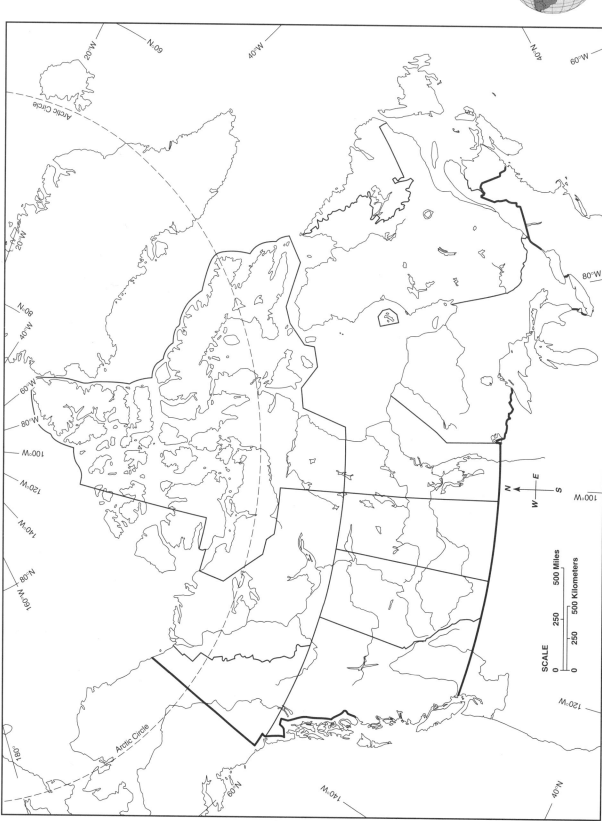

Name _____ Class _____ Date _____

Mexico

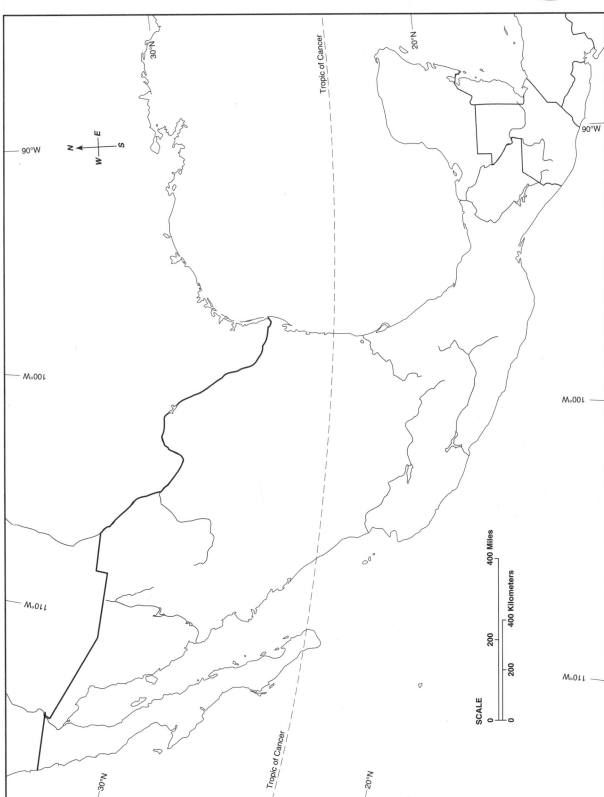

Name _____ Class _____ Date _____

Central America and the Caribbean

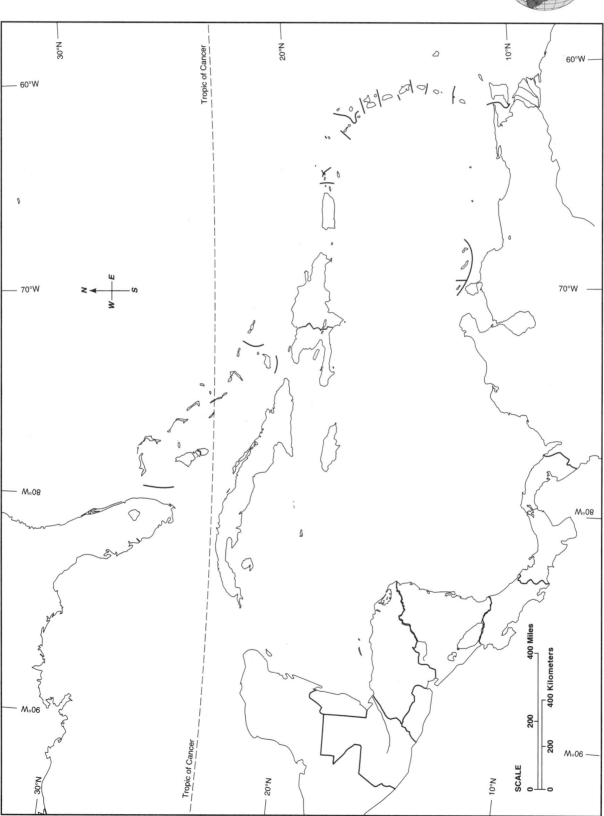

OUTLINE MAP 13

South America

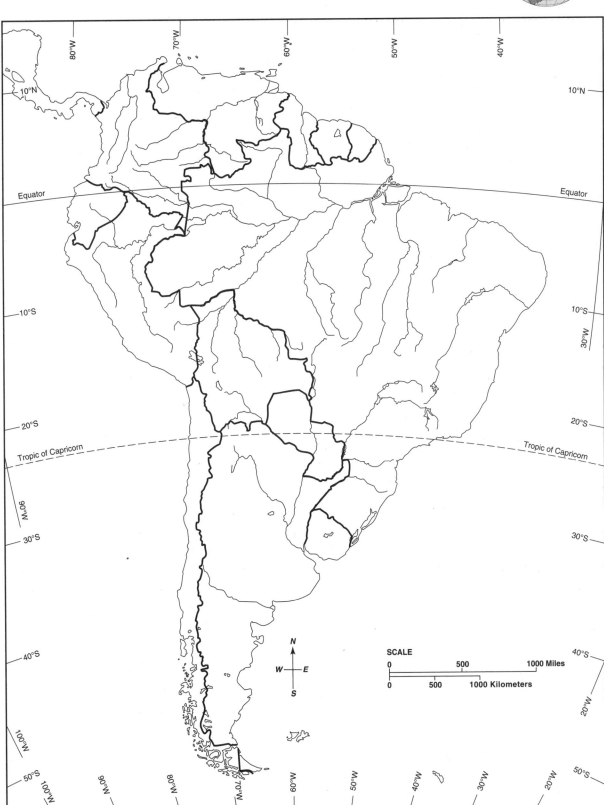

10°N

Equator

10°S

20°S

Tropic of Capricorn

30°S

40°S

50°S

80°W
70°W
60°W
50°W
40°W
30°W
20°W

SCALE

N
W — E
S

0   500   1000 Miles
0   500   1000 Kilometers

OUTLINE MAP 14
Europe

SCALE

0   250   500 Miles

0   250   500 Kilometers

Name _____ Class _____ Date _____

SCALE

0 _____ 250 _____ 500 Miles

0 _____ 250 _____ 500 Kilometers

OUTLINE MAP 16

Russia and Northern Eurasia

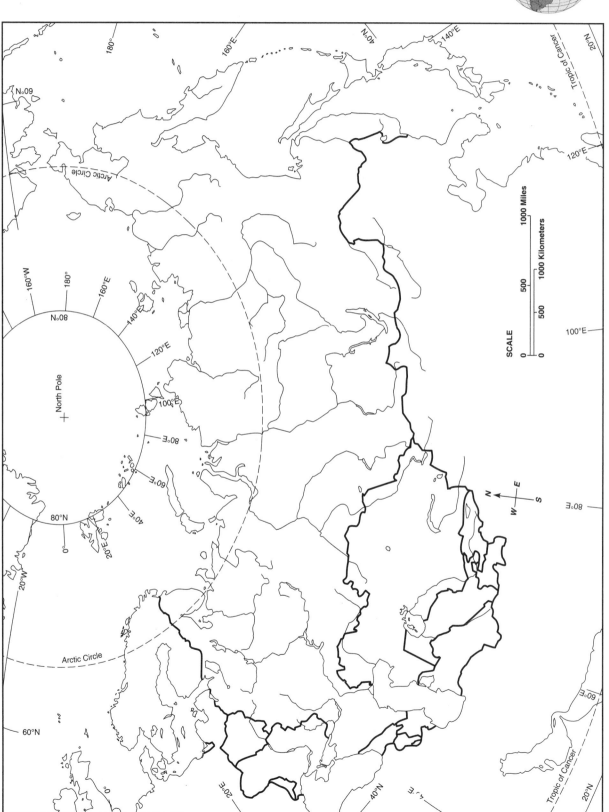

OUTLINE MAP 17
Southwest Asia

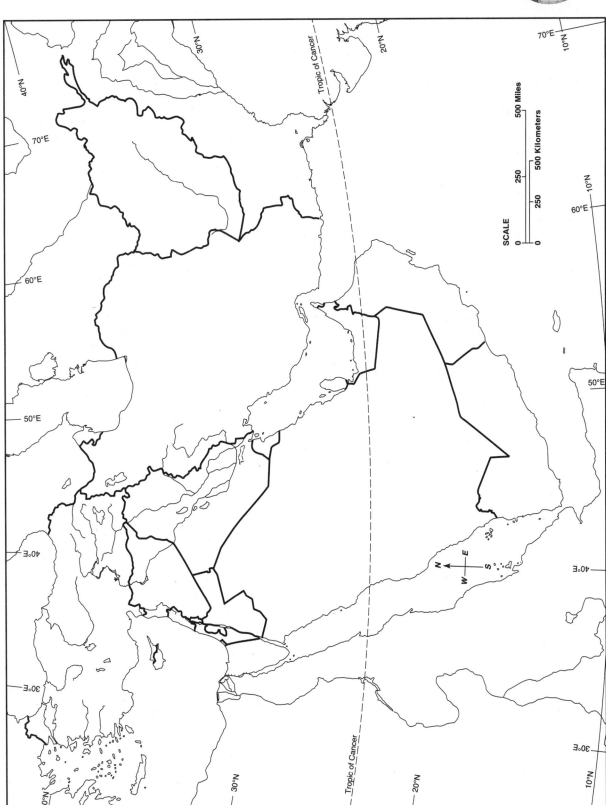

Name _____ Class _____ Date _____

Eastern Mediterranean

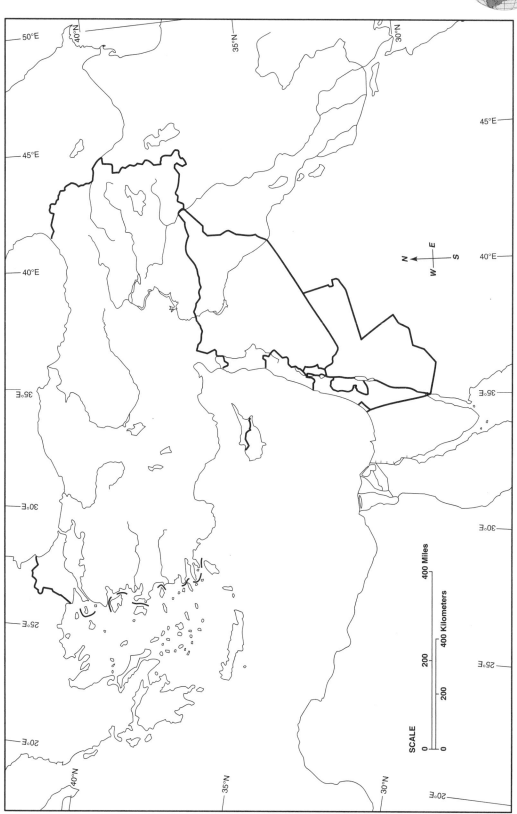

50°E
40°N
35°N
30°N
45°E
45°E
40°E
40°E
35°E
35°E
30°E
30°E
25°E
25°E
20°E
40°N
35°N
30°N
20°E

N
E
W
S

SCALE

400 Miles

200

0

400 Kilometers

200

0

OUTLINE MAP 19

Africa

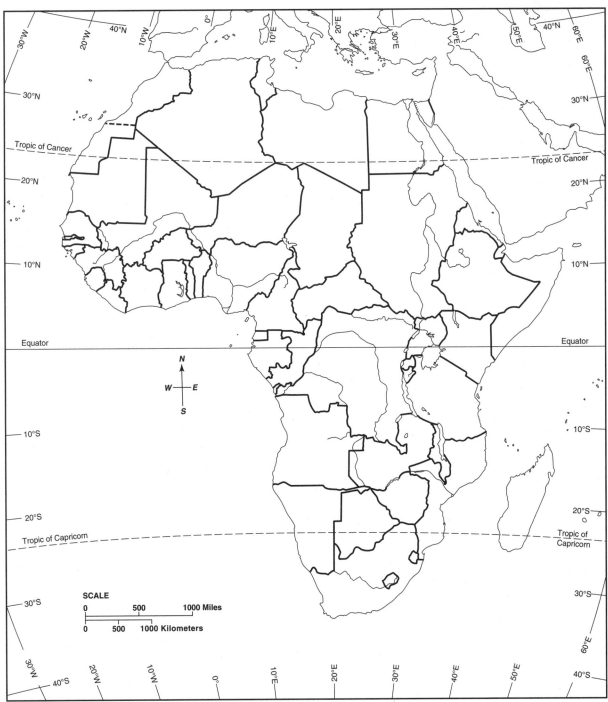

Tropic of Cancer

Tropic of Cancer

Equator

Equator

Tropic of Capricorn

Tropic of Capricorn

SCALE

0   500   1000 Miles

0   500   1000 Kilometers

Name _____ Class _____ Date _____

East Asia

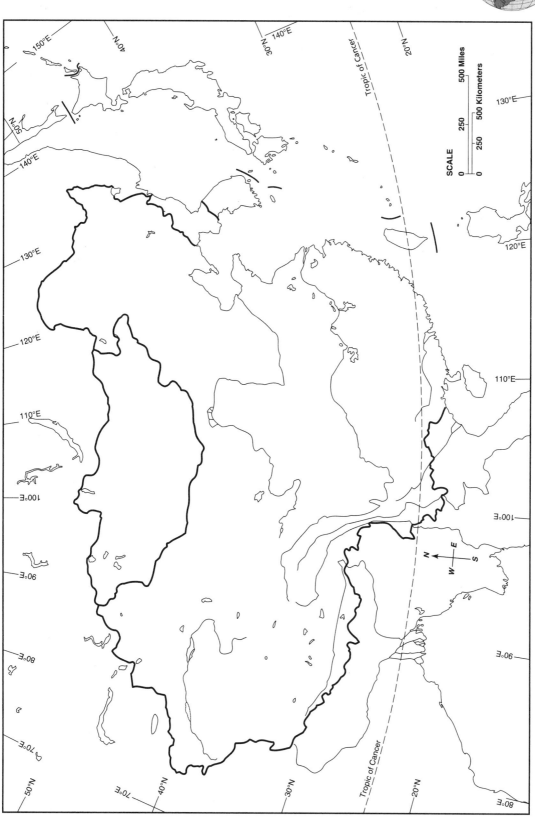

SCALE

500 Miles

250

0

500 Kilometers

250

0

Tropic of Cancer

OUTLINE MAP 21

Southeast Asia

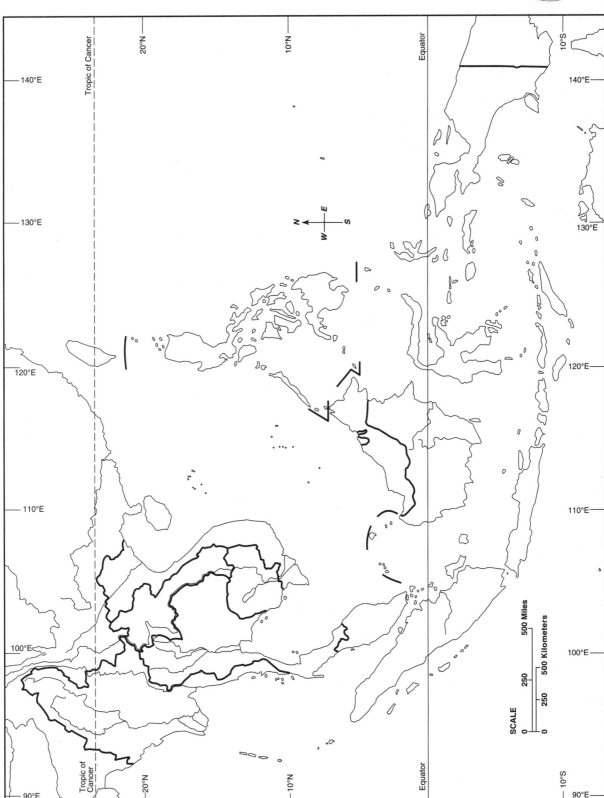

Name _____ Class _____ Date _____

OUTLINE MAP 22
South Asia

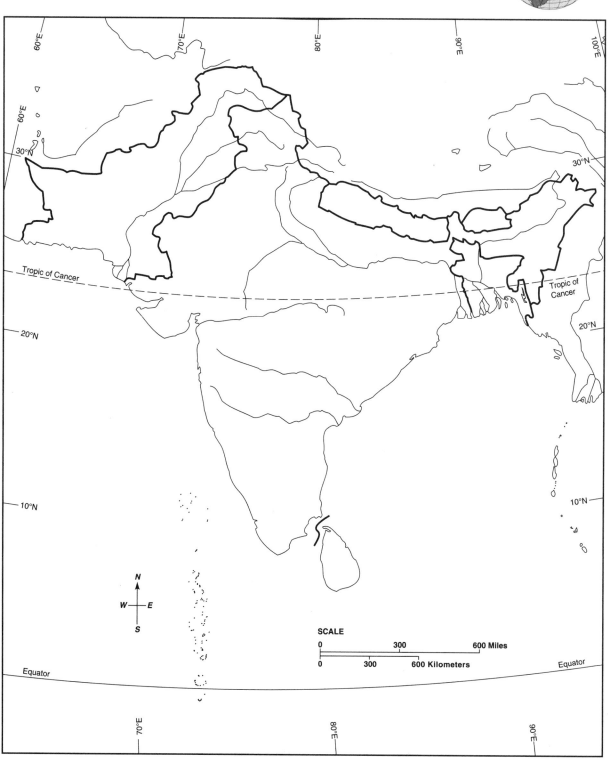

OUTLINE MAP 23
Australia and New Zealand

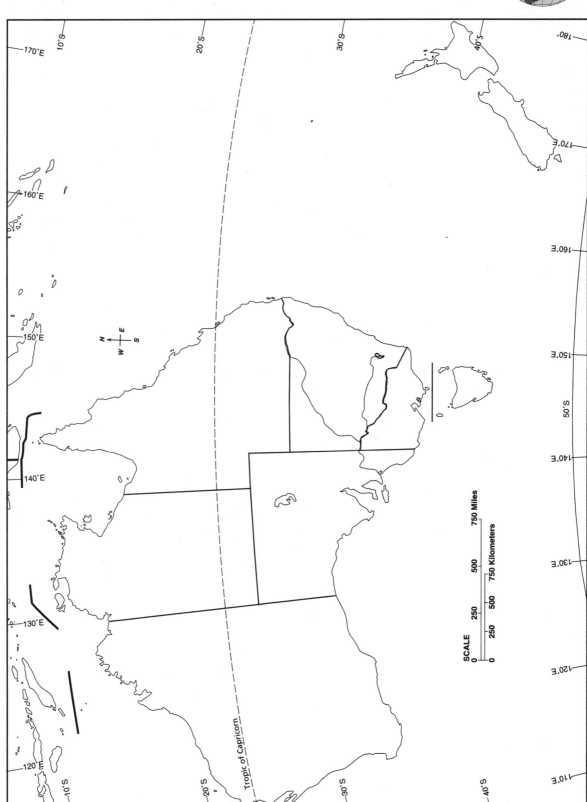

170°E
160°E
150°E
140°E
130°E
120°E

10°S
20°S
30°S
40°S

10°S
20°S
30°S
40°S

180°
170°E
160°E
150°E
140°E
130°E
120°E
110°E

50°S

N
E
S
W

Tropic of Capricorn

SCALE
0   250   500   750 Miles
0   250   500   750 Kilometers

OUTLINE MAP 24

The Pacific Rim

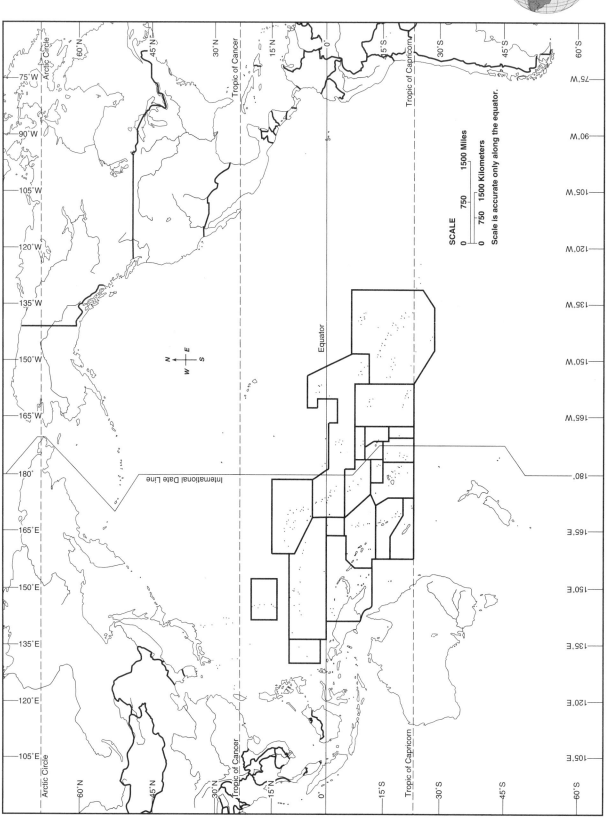

SCALE

0   750   1500 Miles

0   750   1500 Kilometers

Scale is accurate only along the equator.

Name _____ Class _____ Date _____

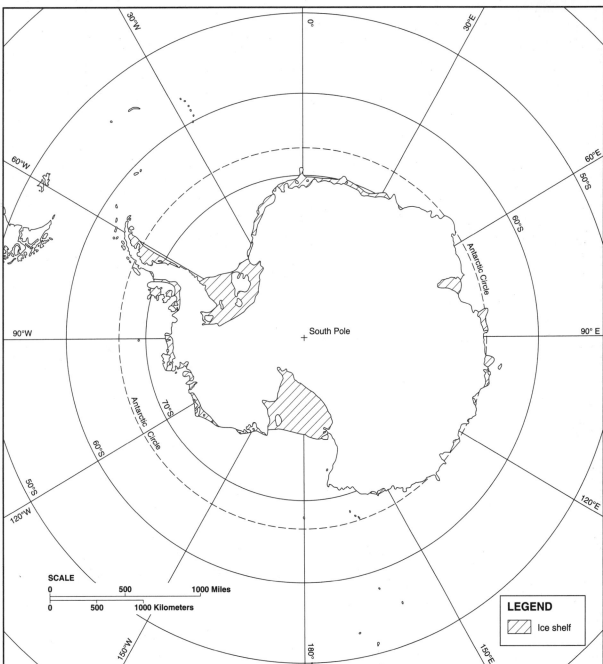

30°W   0°   30°E

60°W   60°E
                        50°S
                        60°S
                        Antarctic Circle

90°W   + South Pole   90° E

Antarctic Circle
70°S
60°S
50°S
120°W   120°E

SCALE
0   500   1000 Miles
0   500   1000 Kilometers

150°W   180°   150°E

LEGEND
/// Ice shelf